DR. PHILLIPS'

MISSIONARY ADDRESS.

A MISSIONARY ADDRESS

BY THE

REV. WILLIAM W. PHILLIPS, D. D.,

MINISTER OF THE FIRST PRESBYTERIAN CHURCH, NEW YORK,

Delivered in Newburgh, Oct. 16, 1860, before the Synod of New York,

BY ITS APPOINTMENT.

PUBLISHED AT THE REQUEST OF THE EXECUTIVE COMMITTEE OF THE BOARD OF FOREIGN MISSIONS OF THE PRESBYTERIAN CHURCH.

NEW YORK:

MISSION HOUSE, No. 23 CENTRE STREET.

1860.

ADDRESS.

The enjoyment of privileges is attended with corresponding obligations. To whom much is given, of them much will be required. We all have our talents, for which we must give an account according to our several ability. God has made us to differ from millions of the human family by giving us the gospel of his grace. He has imparted to us this good, not for our sakes only, but that we may impart it to others, accompanying it with the injunction, "Freely ye have received, freely give." The commission which was given by our Lord to his disciples, after his resurrection, "Go ye into all the world and preach the gospel to every creature," is binding on the whole church, on every individual to whom the gospel comes. They must not hide it, nor attempt to monopolize it, but must diffuse it, and let the light of it shine as freely and as extensively as the light of the sun. Our Lord has displayed much wisdom and great mercy in this arrangement. He might have accomplished his object in other ways, without employing human agency; but he has conferred a rich blessing and a high honor on those to whom he sends the gospel, by requiring them to propagate it, and making them co-workers with himself, whilst he thus receives all the glory of its success, by putting the treasure of the gospel in earthen vessels, that the excellency of the power may be manifestly of him. He at the same time calls into exercise the grace he has communicated to his servants through its instrumentality, and thus perfects their Christian character. He permits them to sympathize with him, to imitate his example, to be transformed into his likeness, and to know in their own experience the truth of the declaration, that "it is more blessed to give than to receive." To be permitted to do good and to communicate, in obedience to the command and in imitation of Jehovah, elevates and purifies the soul, satisfies its longings, and fills it with peace and joy, which are peculiar and divine. To enlighten the ignorant, to elevate the degraded, to reclaim the wandering, to save the lost, to be instrumental in quickening the dead in trespasses and in sins, and in making them heirs of eternal life, by making known to them the living and true God, and Jesus Christ whom he hath sent—is an employment worthy of an immortal soul, and appropriate for a redeemed spirit. It has connected with it the highest recompense that can be bestowed on earth or in heaven. "They that turn many to righteousness shall shine as the stars forever and ever."

The distinction between home and foreign missions was not so recognized in the New Testament as to give any priority or preponderance to either. Our Lord distinctly declared, that the field was the world. The souls which were to be gathered into his fold, were those which had been given him by the Father, and had been redeemed by him. They were on different parts of the globe, and most of them yet to be born. For special reasons the apostles were required to commence their ministry at Jerusalem; but it was not to end there, nor would God allow them to remain there until every individual in that city should have been converted. He permitted a violent persecution to arise, by which they were dispersed and driven away, to preach the gospel every where. God makes those to whom he gives the gospel debtors to the Jews and to the Greeks, to the barbarians, Scythians, bond and free. None are to be overlooked nor to be neglected, since all are included in the commission. As we cannot occupy the whole field at once, having neither the men nor the means to do so; as there ever have been some portions of the field closed against the introduction of the gospel; as the early disciples were directed, when persecuted in one city, to flee to another, and to turn away altogether from those who refused to receive them, and who rejected the gospel peremptorily,—we are authorized to ask counsel of God, to follow the leadings of his providence, and to exercise our best judgment according to the light which may be given us, in the immediate selection of our particular fields from among those which are open to us. But we are not to be influenced by our own preferences or biassed reasons, by any selfish considerations of the inconvenience, difficulties, and sacrifices which may attend the enterprise. Nor are we to decide as to the probabilities of success as they may appear to us, in one place rather than in another, by the judgment of sense, to the exclusion of faith in the promise of the presence of God with us. Least of all should we array one field against another as rivals, since all are to be cultivated, and the work is one. We must remember how incompetent we are to interpret the indications of providence; how liable we are to mistake the import and design of what are regarded as adverse providences; and therefore we must not make them alone the rule of our action, but consider them in connection with his Word and the promised guidance of his Spirit. We must not forget that God designs to try the faith of his people, to test their sincerity, and the strength of their attachment to him and to his cause. He has not promised to grant us, invariably, immediate and uninterrupted success when we engage in his work. The history of missions reveals the fact, that in some instances where the church has been called to make the greatest and most painful sacrifices, and to wait longest for fruit, she has reaped the most abundant harvest.

The men of the world ask, Why send the gospel to those who speak other languages which must with difficulty be acquired by our missionaries, at great cost of time, labor, and means? Why send to those who do not desire to have the gospel, and cannot appreciate it, and who, perhaps, will abuse, persecute, and murder the messengers of the churches,—especially when we have so many destitute of the means of grace, ignorant and perishing, among ourselves; so many who speak our own language, and who live where the prospect of success in preaching the gospel is so much more promising? This question meets us constantly: it is reiterated from week to week. Whenever cases of extreme destitution are brought to the knowledge of the public, we are reminded that it would be far better to relieve these than to send missionaries to the heathen, as if doing so were the cause of the destitution, and as if doing both were inconsistent with each other. The question is asked by some insidiously and maliciously, not because they care for the poor, but because they hate Christianity, are hostile to its propagation any where, and would, if they could, prevent it altogether. We are tempted to ask this class of objectors, If the attempt to save the heathen of other lands is so hopeless and absurd as they represent it to be; if it must from necessity soon be abandoned; if those who are engaged in it must sooner or later discover their mistake,—why then should those who take no interest in it be so exercised about it? What is it to them? They are at perfect liberty to withhold their co-operation.

This question is also asked by others in good faith, but, as we think, through a want of consideration and a misapprehension of the subject. We must therefore continue to answer it, though it has been repeatedly answered. We believe the question is founded on utterly false assumptions.

First: It is taken for granted that the work is of man, and not of God; that it is optional, not obligatory; that the church may engage in it, or not, as she may think best; that we are to exercise our own judgment and discretion respecting it, as we do about the enterprises of this world, and may be governed by expediency in deciding the question of our duty respecting it. It overlooks the great fact that it is God's work, required by him, and to be accomplished by him through our instrumentality. He has enjoined the performance of this duty on all his servants, individually and collectively; they have no discretion respecting it; neither can they evade the obligation to engage in it, whilst they are reminded that it is to be accomplished "not by might, nor by power, but by his Spirit." Human wisdom is utterly incompetent to judge concerning it, being folly in God's estimation. It is not a matter of dollars and cents, nor of expediency, nor of comfort and convenience. The difficulties in the way of its performance, or the sacrifices it may require, are to have no weight in deciding the question of our duty respecting it. God has purposed to gather into his fold a multitude which no man can number, out of every nation and kindred and people and tongue under the whole heaven. These have been given to Christ, and have been redeemed by him, and must be gathered into his fold as the travail of his soul, and at last presented to the Father without spot, and blameless. They all must have their robes made white in the blood of the Lamb. "The heathen have been given to Christ for his inheritance, and the uttermost parts of the earth for his possession." "To him every knee shall bow, and every tongue confess that he is Lord, to the glory of God." "All nations shall serve him." "The ends of the earth shall see his salvation." "The kingdoms of this world shall become the kingdom of our Lord, and of his Christ." All the glorious things that have been written of the city of our God shall be realized. All that has been promised to Christ as "the Light to lighten the Gentiles, as well as the glory of his people Israel," as head over all things unto the church, shall be fulfilled, and that through the preaching of the gospel. The fact that the heathen do not desire the gospel, being ignorant of it, is the strongest proof of their need of it. The greater their blindness, the more deplorable their ignorance, the more urgent is their call for the gospel. Our ancestors did not desire it, and had they been left to themselves neither they nor any of their descendants would ever have desired it.

We must remember, that whilst there may be greater external and apparent obstacles in the way of the success of the gospel in one field than in another, and in the case of some individuals than of others, the state of the human heart with respect to God and his Christ, is the same in all: all souls are by nature dead in trespasses and sins; and all hearts are alike shut against the gospel, and alienated from the life of God. The carnal mind everywhere is enmity against God. "The natural man receiveth not the things of the Spirit of God; they are foolishness unto him; neither can he know them, because they are spiritually discerned." It requires the same power to convert the wisest, most intelligent, learned, refined, amiable, and estimable citizen of a civilized community, which is necessary to convert the dullest, most stupid, ignorant, debased, and defiled heathen. That power must come from God, who is as able and as willing to exert it in the one case as in the other. As for having heathen near us, there will be such in all nominally Christian lands until the end of time. The tares are allowed to grow with the wheat until harvest.

It is necessary to reiterate these elementary and fundamental truths, and to remind the people, from time to time, that God requires them personally to love their neighbor as themselves, and, in imitation of the example of Christ, to do good, to seek and to save the lost, or we cannot expect their cordial coöperation in the work of spreading the gospel. To do this is very far from being preposterous; it is not even a doubtful experiment. The gospel has been proved adequate as a remedy in every case, both to the Jew and also to the Gentile. "It is the wisdom of God, and the power of God unto salvation to every one that believes." The obstacles which were overcome by it, in the days of the apostles, were greater than any that have existed since. Its success in the pagan Roman empire, and in the Grecian heathen cities, was an earnest of its success in all time, and among all nations. Nor can it be preached in vain; it shall accomplish that to which it is sent. Sooner or later it will prove a savor of life unto life, or of death unto death, to all who hear it. We may preach it among ourselves, where outward circumstances seem to favor its reception, and where appearances seem to promise certain success, and yet be disappointed as to the immediate fruits of it; and this is the worst that can happen to us in preaching it among the heathen. The success must come from God, everywhere. "Paul may plant, and Apollos water, but God must give the increase."

In view of these truths, then, why should we make a difference between home and foreign missions, and prefer the field at home; more especially as God has so greatly blessed the labors of his servants in the foreign field, granting them equal if not greater success, in proportion to the means used, than to his servants at home?

Secondly: Another false assumption implied in the question is, that the exportation of the men and means sent abroad to preach the gospel, is a diminution to that amount of, and a subtraction from, the available men and means at home. It is alleged that we cannot spare them from the home field, as the demand for them here is greater than we can supply. This too is a mistake. It the first place, it is not true that all the men who have gone to the foreign field would have been laborers in the home field had they not been sent abroad. Some of then had been given to the Lord for that specific service by their parents, and others were so drawn to it as to choose it exclusively. They would not have been in the ministry at all if they could not have been ordained as foreign missionaries. Neither is it true that all the funds, which have been contributed to give the gospel to the heathen, would have been available for domestic missions, if the foreign field had been overlooked. Men have their preferences, and their own peculiar views of duty, and of their responsibility to God as stewards of the goods entrusted to them. The inference is gratuitous, that because they are willing to give to an object which they appreciate highly, they would have given the same to another object more worthy, it may be, if the first had been withdrawn.

We might as well say, How much better it would be to appropriate to some benevolent object those large sums which are uselessly expended for shows and exhibitions, for extravagant and luxurious entertainments. But would they be thus appropriated if they were not thus squandered? In the next place, experience has taught us, in confirmation of the doctrine taught in the Word of God, that this exportation of men and means, in obedience to the command of Christ, and to promote his glory among the heathen, exerts a most salutary influence, and produces a most favorable reaction on the church, increasing her piety and her resources. We view the operation of this movement, by faith. We look with confidence to God, who can, and who does, raise up ten in the room of every one who is sent abroad, and who can cause the good seed thus sown to bring forth thirty, sixty, and an hundred-fold. It is especially true in this case, as in all matters by which God is honored, that they who scatter do yet increase, whilst the withholding of more than is meet tendeth to poverty. When or where has any church been made poorer and weaker by parting with some of her members and of her substance for the benefit of the destitute and the lost? Nay, the church which adopts the blind and selfish policy of limiting her benevolent operations to her own immediate wants—of monopolizing, circumscribing, and withholding her resources, will experience a stagnation in her gifts and graces, and a gradual drying up of her springs of life and energy. Her faith, her love, her sympathies, are not called into full exercise; her heart does not beat in unison with Christ; she does not manifest his mind and spirit, nor does she follow him wholly. We would ask the churches engaged in this work, which hold their solemn and interesting concerts of prayer in connection with it, when they feel that God is with them and honoring them, granting them seasons of refreshing from his presence,—could they do without those services, or would they willingly consent to be deprived of their influence?

There need be no apprehensions lest the contributions for the salvation of the perishing heathen will diminish those for other benevolent objects. They are means, under God, of drawing out the resources of the church, and of strengthening her for the work of the Lord. Hence we feel that when we are advocating the cause of foreign missions we are at the same time most effectually promoting domestic missions, on the principle that they who water others shall themselves be watered. The one cannot be prosecuted successfully, or prosper, without the other. Instead of attempting to estimate the comparative importance of the various objects contemplated by our church, or of preferring one before the other, we regard them as identical, and of equal importance, each in its place. We must have churches at home on which to rely, under God, for the means of doing his work. These must furnish, train up, and send forth the ministry, the missionaries, and the various agents for the spread of the gospel, with the supplies required for their support. To do any thing that should cripple these churches, impede their progress, or diminish their numbers, would be suicidal. We must have schools, colleges, and theological seminaries under their respective boards, for educating the men who have been called of God to go forth into the world, which is the field to be cultivated, and to be brought into subjection to Christ. These institutions are so intimately connected, so mutually dependent and helpful to each other, that you cannot neglect the one without injuriously affecting the others. Those who are the true and intelligent friends of any one of them are the reliable friends of the whole. Being taught by the Spirit, they feel that they cannot fully develop their Christian character, grow in grace, abound in all good works, exercise the Christian affections, and enjoy the pure and holy emotions of sanctified spirits in Christ, nor meet their responsibility to God, without sustaining them all by their prayers and benefactions, since they are all aiming at the same end, and engaged in different departments of the same work.

We think it will not be denied, however, that a sincere and

ardent desire for the salvation of the heathen, such a love for their souls, such a desire for their redemption to the glory of God, as makes men willing to devote themselves to the service of Christ in their behalf by going personally—leaving home, and kindred, and country, or enabling others to go to them, because they are perishing, and because the name of God is blasphemed among them,—is a higher attainment than a simple willingness to devote one's self to the ministry at home, or to contribute to the support and spread of the gospel among ourselves. We do not now speak of the comparative piety of the ministry at home and abroad, nor of the comparative sacrifices and privations which fall to the lot of each respectively. No doubt the foreign missionary may deceive himself as to his motives and views as easily as the other, and no doubt the domestic missionary may suffer as great or greater privations than the other. But the spirit of which we speak is more unselfish and disinterested, and has in it less mixture of motives than may actuate some in entering the ministry for the domestic field. There are no considerations of personal advantage to be derived from the foreign mission, to influence any one to undertake it. He who devotes himself to it does not go from love of country, from any feelings of pride, or from expectations of promoting personal comfort, or private interests in elevating public sentiment in the community, and in strengthening the civil and social bonds of the society of which he is a member,—some of which would be proper motives for exercising the ministry at home. But he professes to be more self-sacrificing and Christ-like, inasmuch as he goes solely for the sake of imparting these blessings, of bringing into operation these motives, and of accomplishing these ends among the heathen. He has respect to the recompense of reward, it is true, but it is wholly to a spiritual and heavenly reward; partaking of the nature of that joy which was set before the Saviour, for which he endured the cross despising the shame.

Let it be remembered, further, that as yet there is much more done for home than for foreign missions. Whilst thousands and millions are contributed for the endowment of schools and colleges, for the building of churches and the establishment of hospitals; whilst immense sums are annually expended for the support of these institutions, for the education of youth, for the training of men for the ministry, for the support of the ministry of the gospel, for Bible, Tract, Sunday-school, and kindred societies, and for the maintenance of the poor,—for all which we bless God, and pray that these expenditures may be continued and enlarged,—a mere pittance is given in one annual contribution of the church, to be applied to the support of all these objects severally and separately among the heathen, who require them as much as we do ourselves. Among us, these have each separate funds for their support, and very properly; among the heathen, they must all be supported out of one single fund. By taking this view of the subject, which is the correct one, we may discover the great disparity between the amounts collected for foreign and for domestic missions. It is natural that men should be more willing to labor for themselves, for their kindred and friends, than for strangers, and to contribute more liberally for objects near and at hand, where, judging from apparent probabilities, they have reason to expect more immediate returns, than for objects at a distance, where fruit can be expected only at a remote period.

We are now prepared to answer the question directly. We send the gospel to the heathen because God has commanded us to do it; because they are destitute of it, are lost without it, and must perish eternally if it be not sent to them. Are not these most weighty and sufficient reasons? We have it among us, and are under unspeakable obligations to God for it. From our childhood we have known the sacred Scriptures, which are able to make us wise unto salvation. Our government, laws, social state, habits of thought and life, have been formed under the influence of the Word of God. We have the Bible, and the means of multiplying and disseminating it. We have the Sabbath, the ministry, the Christian family, the church with all her agencies. By the blessing of God, these will be preserved in the field at home, and will accomplish their benevolent work. The good seed has been sown broadcast in our midst and around us, and is springing up on every side. The leaven is working, and will permeate the whole mass. There is not an individual in the whole land who may not have access to some one, or all, of those means of salvation.

With the heathen it is not so. They have not the gospel, nor can they obtain it, unless it be carried to them. It will not spring up from the soil; it will not be sent to them from heaven. There will be no new or further revelation to the children of men; nor can they discover its truths by their own reasonings. Being without the knowledge which the gospel alone imparts, they are hopelessly lost. It is important that we should have our minds fully and deeply impressed with this melancholy and alarming truth. The practical unbelief of it is very prevalent, and occasions listlessness on this subject, and the want of missionary zeal and exertion. Many will not believe that all who are without the gospel must be lost. They cherish a secret impression that, in some way, the heathen may be saved without the gospel. Some, as an excuse for their neglect of them, willingly persuade themselves that this is possible. Without attempting to pry into the secret counsels of God, or indulging in our own conjectures of what God may do with the heathen, we must confine ourselves to his Word as the only source of our knowledge and the only rule of our faith on this subject. Here we learn that, whilst they will not be condemned for their unbelief, yet they are condemned. "They that sin without law shall perish without law." Having been left without a revelation, or rather having sinned it away, they are a law unto themselves, and are without excuse. They do not use the light which they have. They do not attain the knowledge of the invisible things of God, which they might acquire from the things which are seen.

As they did not like to retain God in their knowledge, they were given up to a reprobate mind. There has never been a single instance in which a heathen has attained the knowledge of the true God, and has been saved from his sins, without the gospel. "If our gospel be hid, it is hid to them that are lost." This is true universally. If from any cause, whether among ourselves or among the heathen, the gospel be not apprehended and appreciated, if it be not believed and obeyed by any, they must be lost; they are left in their sins under condemnation, to perish eternally. "The name of Jesus is the only name given under heaven among men whereby we can be saved." The Saviour hath said, "This is life eternal, to know thee, the only living and true God, and Jesus Christ whom thou hast sent." The heathen are without this knowledge. It is written also, "Without holiness no man shall see the Lord." "There shall in no wise enter into his kingdom any thing that defileth, or worketh abomination, or maketh a lie." Has there ever been a holy heathen; or is there one holy person anywhere among those who either have not the gospel or have rejected it? At the same time it is universally true, and will be to the end of time, that "Whosoever shall call on the name of the Lord shall be saved. How, then, shall they call on him in whom they have not believed? and how shall they believe in him of whom they have not heard? and how shall they hear without a preacher? and how shall they preach except they be sent?" Therefore have we been required to preach the gospel to every creature; and we are required to do it out of regard to our God, that we may honor him, and make him known to others, who may unite with us in vindicating his dealings with the children of men, and secure to him the glory which is due unto his name. He asks, "If I be a father, where is mine honor? if I be a master, where is my fear?" Not only is he not known among the heathen, not only does he not receive the tribute of praise which is due unto him from the immense mass of immortal minds which he has created, but his name is blasphemed among them. He is misrepresented, vilified, and dishonored. What evidence do we give that we are his disciples, or that we love him, if we care not for this state of things, if we disobey his last and parting command, or if we manifest no zeal or jealousy for his honor,—if we simply pray, Hallowed be thy name, thy kingdom come, and do nothing to make him known or to extend his kingdom? Besides, do we owe him nothing for the gift of his Son to be our Saviour, for the gospel of his grace? Have we no sympathy for the heathen, who are members of the same human family with us? The return required of us for our distinguished benefits, conferred and enjoyed through the gospel, is, that we should impart them to others,—that we should do good with them to our fellow-men.

Now, the great encouragement we have to engage in this work, and which precludes every excuse for its neglect, is the certainty of its success. It is not a Utopian scheme. We are not called to fight uncertainly, as men beating the air. Our work of faith and labor of love for the heathen cannot be in vain in the Lord. This certainty is founded on the covenant transaction between the Father and the Son. God the Father gave a people to the Son, to be redeemed by him; as the Son declared in his intercessory prayer: "Thine they were, and thou gavest them me." The Son has complied with the terms on which the promises of that covenant were made, and can claim their fulfilment. Having made his soul an offering for sin, he shall see of the travail of his soul and be satisfied: he shall see his seed. "The earth shall be full of the knowledge of the Lord;" "all flesh shall see the salvation of God." The mouth of the Lord hath spoken it.

It is remarkable that the inquiry of certain Greeks after Jesus was the occasion of directing the mind of the Saviour specially to this great subject. We read in John xii., 20–23, that when he was told that certain Greeks desired to see him, he answered them saying, "The hour is come that the Son of man should be glorified. Verily, verily, I say unto you, except a corn of wheat fall into the ground and die, it abideth alone; but if it die it bringeth forth much fruit." The hour of his conflict with the powers of darkness, and of his penal death as the price of our redemption, was at hand—the hour of trial and of great darkness to himself and to his disciples; therefore he adds, in view of it, "He that loveth his life shall lose it, and he that hateth his life in this world shall keep it unto life eternal. If any man serve me, let him follow me; and where I am there shall also my servant be. If any man serve me, him will my Father honor." He felt that both he and his disciples required to be strengthened by these considerations: "Now is my soul troubled; and what shall I say? Father, save me from this hour? But for this cause came I unto this hour. Father, glorify thy name!"—vindicate the honor of thy name!—satisfy all the demands of thy law and the claims of justice! Here I am, a willing victim, waiting to pay the ransom-price. Now is the judgment of this world. Now the question is to be decided, whether this world is to be redeemed; whether it shall be wrested from the power of Satan, and restored to its rightful proprietor. Now shall the prince of this world be cast out; his interests shall be condemned, his power broken, that the time may come when he will deceive the nations no more. "And I, if I be lifted up, will draw all men unto me."

We know what followed. He consented not to be saved from that hour, and that the wrath and curse of God should come upon him to the uttermost. He submitted to every form of humiliation, degradation, and suffering; to the agony of the garden, which caused his sweat, as it were great drops of blood, to fall to the ground, and caused him to pray three times, saying the same words: "Father! if it be possible, let this cup pass from me!" He submitted to desertion by his Father, and the accursed death of the cross, which were the procuring cause of our redemption. The cup did not pass from him: he drank it. The Father did not spare him, but delivered him up for us all. It pleased the Lord to bruise him. He was denied by his disciples; despised, rejected, and set at naught by his own nation; delivered into the hands of the Gentiles to be condemned; buffeted, spit upon, crowned with thorns, and nailed to the cross. While suspended there, he was treated with every indignity by the vilest instruments, and experienced the withdrawal of the light of his Father's countenance, and the privation of that sensible aid, strength, and comfort from him, which he had enjoyed hitherto, extorting from him that piercing and heart-rending cry: "My God! my God! why hast thou forsaken me?" Thus he put himself in the condition, and in the room, of those whom he came to redeem. He suffered all which they had deserved to suffer, and in their stead, "the just for the unjust, that he might bring us to God." For "the joy that was set before him, he endured the cross, despising the shame;" and that joy was, to see God glorified, and his redeemed, regenerated and sanctified, presented to the Father as the children who had been given him, and as his inheritance. And can it be, that after all they shall not be delivered, that he shall fail to receive his reward, and be disappointed? Among men, this might be; and if any thing in this arrangement depended upon men, such a thing might be; but with God, it cannot be. The covenant has been ratified with the oath of God, and cannot be broken. The Lord Jesus Christ, as the surety of the covenant, had his reward as well as his work before him. Having performed his work, and fully complied with all the conditions of the covenant, he must receive his reward. His people shall be made willing in the day of his power, and be gathered into his fold, and that through the preaching of the gospel to them by those who have received it. If we decline the work, it will be done by other hands; whilst we shall lose the opportunity and the honor.

I stand here not to instruct you. I say these things not because you do not know them, but to put you in remembrance of them, and because he, who has been working hitherto and is still working, calls us to-day, more loudly than he has ever done, to make greater sacrifices for Christ, to engage with more diligence in his service, and to pray with more fervor than we have ever done for the ingathering of his elect. He has been removing lets and hinderances out of our way, and has opened doors by which his Word may enter, have free course, and be glorified. Behold what God hath wrought in our day! How many great and precious promises to the church have been fulfilled! How much of his gracious and glorious purpose have we been permitted to see accomplished! The Pagan power, the Mohammedan power, and the Papal power, so long since doomed, have been weakened and so nearly destroyed as no longer to stand in the way of the propagation of the gospel. Africa has been explored: her extended territory, her vast resources, her immense population, the comparative healthfulness of her climate, have been brought to light. India is more open than she has ever been. China, we have reason to hope, will soon be open throughout her length and breadth. Italy, where so recently the possession of the word of God, or the reading and hearing of it, was regarded as a crime, and punished with imprisonment,—despotic and idolatrous Italy, which gloried in the terrors of the Inquisition,—is now open to the introduction of the gospel. The ten horns of the beast are beginning to hate the woman seated upon the seven hills, and to make her desolate and naked. Now, in this crisis of their history, now, when there is such a tide in their affairs to be improved, it is incumbent on the people of God to enter with an army of missionaries, and with an abundant supply of Bibles, to meet the wants of those millions who have been so long suffering and perishing from a famine of the Word of God. Let not their spiritual emancipation be delayed through our default,—we speak after the manner of men. The children of Israel, humanly speaking, might have been delivered from their bondage, and might have sooner entered the promised land, but for their blindness, perverseness, and unbelief. And they might have taken possession of the whole land immediately after their entrance into Canaan, but for their spiritual sloth and disobedience. Let us discern the signs of the times, recognize the hand of God, hear his voice, and learn from his Word and providence what he will have us to do. Let us live "looking for and hasting unto the coming of the day of God." Then "the kingdom and dominion and the greatness of the kingdom under the whole heaven shall be given to the people of the saints of the Most High, whose kingdom is an everlasting kingdom, and all dominions shall serve and obey him."

This work in foreign lands has become dearer to us on account of what it has already cost us,—even the many precious lives of those who went for us as our representatives. Our brethren and sisters are there. Our children have gone there. Having invested so much in it, we cannot afford to abandon it. We must go forward, and continue to prosecute it. The young, amiable, and estimable, the learned, accomplished, and devoted, who gave promise of great usefulness, have sacrificed their lives in it. A noble, disinterested, and enviable company, of faithful and self-denying laborers, have fallen in those distant heathen lands; and shall we abandon their graves, and lose all the fruit of their labors? They have speedily accomplished their work; they have early received their crown and entered into their rest; yet they never regretted, nor do they now regret, their mission to the heathen. Those who do not here know why they were thus removed, disappointing the hopes of their friends and of the church, and depriving the heathen of their ministry, shall know hereafter. Has not the church been rebuked for her unbelief, and for having restrained prayer, by her faithful servants having been taken from the evil to come on earth to serve their Lord in heaven? We have lost their labors, but not their life nor their death. These continue to teach us the great and increasing interest we have in this enterprise, and our entire dependence on God for its success; whilst they cease not to appeal most solemnly and tenderly to others to fill their places, to enter upon their labors, and to come to the help of the Lord against the mighty.

www.ingramcontent.com/pod-product-compliance
Lightning Source LLC
LaVergne TN
LVHW011146110826
845150LV00008B/2532

9781418192310